Round and Round the Seasons Go

Round and round

the seasons go.

Winter comes,

cold, white snow.

Round and round

the seasons go.

Spring comes,

flowers grow.

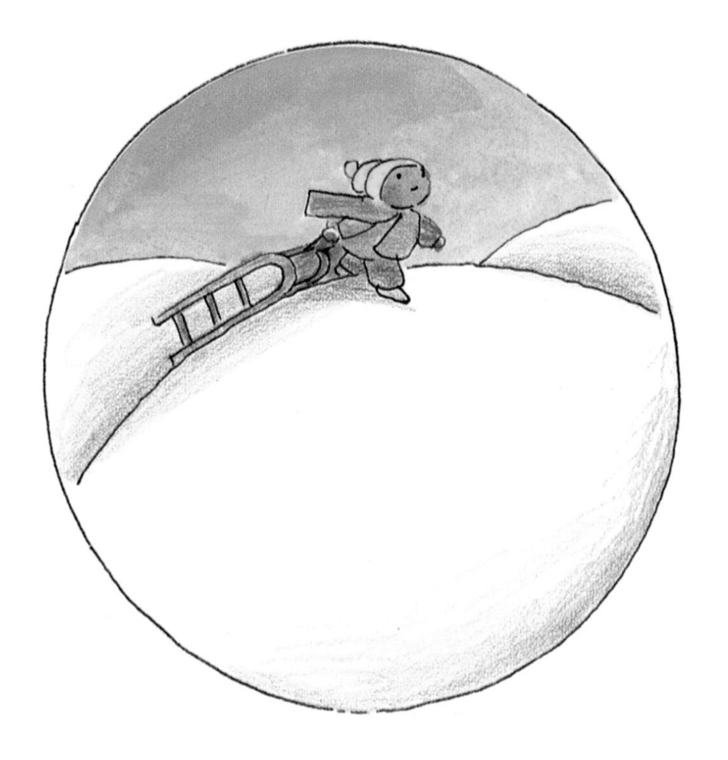

Round and round

the seasons go.

Summer comes,

hot and slow.

Round and round

the seasons go.

Fall comes, leaves blow!